Lotus Petals

Lotus Petals
by Julie MacAdam
© 2022 Julie MacAdam

Cover photo by Zoltan Tasi
https://unsplash.com/@zoltantasi

No part of this book may be used or reproduced by any means, graphic, electronic, or mechanical, including photocopying, recording, taping, or by any information storage retrieval system without the written permission of the publisher except in the case of brief quotations embodied in critical articles and reviews.

ISBN 978-0-9937911-9-2

encreLibre Publishing
Riondel, BC
Canada
encrelibre.com

Lotus Petals

Poems by Julie MacAdam

For Swami Radha -
A Woman with a Vision and the Courage to Listen

Thank you.
For the voice of wisdom within.
Om Saraswati Ma!

These poems were written during my stay at Yasodhara Ashram located on the unceded territory of Ktunaxa and Sinixt peoples. In 2020 I participated in a three month Yoga intensive called the Yoga Development Course which continues to influence the way I teach, learn and live. During the course writing was a way for me to try and give voice to what was happening inside in a form I could later look back upon. The poems are a mix of dreams, waking life experiences and my hearts guidance. Please feel free to substitute your word, or no word, for what you may or may not believe in if Divine Mother does not resonate. I offer my gratitude to my family and the home where I began to write and pray; where I learned poetry is a form of prayer for me. Thank you to my parents for always supporting me to become who I am and to follow the path that suits me. Thanks to my love, Patrick Lambdin, for listening to many poems and supporting me to be my best self and for introducing me to the ashram! To my friends and co-poets along the way; your words and expressions inspire me. To the many writers that keep me going, that are like morning pages full of inspiration, that give voice to the voiceless and the human predicament. Thank you! Thank you to Yasodhara Ashram - for your continued leadership and existence, for your love and celebration of creativity, and for all of you there and all that come and go - our actions and interactions, the practices and teachings are so much a part of these book. I am so grateful to have found my way there.

May we each find our way back home to authenticity. May we each know we are loved. May we each do our good work in this world and walk together in solidarity.

Confidence Hiding / Shames Out

I am the one who went searching for contentment and kept finding desire around each curve of my mind.
I am the one who went looking for love but it was only attachment that I would find.
I am the one who went searching deep inside, for the place in myself where the Truth abides, and I found along the way all those parts of me that hide and lie and try and try.
I am the one that went searching for something still where I can simply be but I was met with all the beliefs that try their best to keep me from being free.
I am the one who went looking for confidence but found self-importance and pride. As I continued to tirely seek it was low-self worth that I'd find although I had long thought it died.
I am the one who went searching for my other half, someone to take my hand but what I know now is that I could never find that in another - woman or man.
Now I see that the seeking and looking kept my eyes blind when with an exhale and an inhale I remember: it is enough to just be and be alive.

That Love

Where is real love?
Is it found somewhere outside of this very heart or reflected
back when given?

Not the kind that looks for its own gratification,
trying to fulfill an endless stream of desire.
Not the kind that is self important, engrossed in me, mine, and
I.
Is that love anyways?
If so, why does my heart break at its presence?

O, where is real love?
That kind of sweet love, the one that flows like Divine nectar.
The love that is complete onto its own self.
The love that knows what will help the lover.
The love that be-friends, cares, and wishes well.

Without a doubt it knows of its' limitlessness and so it offers,
freely, from abundance,
without hesitation because love loves to love.
Where is that love?

That love – children know it and we forget in our performance
art,
in our twisting, our contortions,
all the ways to try to gain and keep love.

Love isn't obtainable.
It is in giving, not grasping, love reveals is omni-presence,
possession doesn't ensure it will stick around.

Love is in action,
it is by being love you know of such.

That love, is the pearl of a great price,
inviting a return to what's essential,
demanding we stop pretending,
that we are less than love.

Keep Going

Once you go forward there is no turning back,
keep going, with poised concentration and a prayer in heart.

Only this, right here,
where there is tension to relax into,
a space worth exploring.

Heart Seed

Inside walls of steel is where my heart was kept,
protected from all things scary and less than perfect.
There, in its' hidden closure, were secret fears of failure.
"Mistakes lead to consequences,
imperfection equates isolation."
Such thoughts shatter worlds.

Lonliness overflows with hope and longing -
Will I make the right choice?
Can I trust my own self?
I don't want to admit my fears, a voice whispers.
It's not who you are, another replies,
hear of your own harborings and hardships;
they aren't much different than mine.

Emerging and becoming is a natural course in time,
seeds follow light,
revealing that absolutely beautiful, absolutely imperfect,
flower.

Without grandiosity or show it is itself.
Authenticity, a choice.

Responsibility

Underwater I found a ring, it had been waiting there for lifetimes.
I know that waiting feeling:
restlessness and dissapointment,
unsettled thoughts of something more,
a search away from the moment.

Grabbing onto an idea, a hope, a dream.
Do I feel well resourced from within?
Do I trust myself?
Divine Mother is in the here and now.

She doesn't arrive with the knight in shining armor,
with vows til death do us part;
She never goes.

It is with recognition that She is revealed;
my responsibility is to remember.

Spider

The spider, she follows me,
there at the door, waiting.
A blackened body with legs close to her center,
I see her now just like in my dreams.

What is this world anyways?
Is it any different then a dream?
What makes it so; can you tell?

I'm still trying to untangle from her web,
she has me caught in strands of love,
a love mysterious and of the finest silk,
intricately catching rays of sun and morning dew.

Her presence calls me to myself,
in a moment of wonder, I ask,
Who are you?
All of your creation, it can be gone in a moment,
is it worth all the effort?

She keeps on going,
Weaving.

Cupid's Ready

There are things that go unspoken yet speak so loudly,
needs never known nor explored, expectations no one agreed to.

In a language beyond words when feeling does the talking,
messages are exchanged and memories revolve in a body.

A certain interest is required to understand,
a willingness worth the effort.
How do you listen?
What do you hear?

If the heart was to speak in subliminial sentences,
would you know what is truly being said?
What does it take to become clear in experiences ever changing?

Committ to an ideal and let it be your arrow.
Cupid is ready.

Deer

There in the middle of the road she stands,
poised, still, looking.

She is received in moments when the reminder to be gentle is
needed most.

With my breathe suspended and scattered,
I slow down and meet her.

Presence is a prerequsit for the attunement it takes to come home,
the arrival to be with this and then that.
Without rush and no sooner, she carries on.

Asking for help, my precious heart quivers,
she is there to meet my eyes with a soft gaze.

It is obvious she is comforted by her integrity,
or perhaps that is my own aspiration.

The Whole

All of me is the offering,
it has to be like that or else my soul goes starving.
It's not a take this and not that kind of play;
Divine Mother is the entirety.

Do flowers hold back when they are ready to bloom?
Choosing which petals to reveal?
The roses, clover, water lillies,
do they think of whether or not to open?

It is Light they are after,
exposing what they are without saying look at me...
But yet we look. We can't help but look.
Authenticity has a drawing power like an opened invitation.

Do you know of your own beauty, they ask.
It isn't alwways pretty yet so precious indeed.
Tell me, would you say my petals should be different?
Why then have such judgment towards yourself?

Everything has meaning and place;
nothing could be wrong with this process of evolution.
It is Light encouraging growth,
from a tender seed to what we become.

We are always becoming, even in dark nights.

Darkened Mother

Therein that darkened stillness,
a place full of movement,
is energy that transforms worlds,
birthing creation unto itself,
destroying what stands in the way of life.

Darkened mother is there,
savaged and hair tossed,
knowing nothing of trying to prove herself;
worth is not a thing that can be proven nor taken away.

She guides me into darkness where there is Light,
that kind of Light revealing shadows she knows how to slay.

With compassion she sees clearly:
there is no one that could give me anything I don't already have;
there is nothing I could offer to others that they are not.

We are everything:
what will you do with such knowledge?

The Work at Hand

I'm not here on this Earth to be liked,
seek approval, or get anything right.
By whose standards?
And who says?

Integrity needs no rules, it moves with heart.
And even if we did, each creates their own;
there is no one size fits all.

Look at the trees,
Oak, Maple, Pine,
are they concerned with their apperance?
Do they try to conform and fit in?
Such vanity is a distraction from the real work at hand.

When looking beyond form it is only the same,
everywhere, the same.
We grow to own our accord.

Birth

Contractions send me towards the floor,
on cool tile I turn sideways looking for a way out,
pain calls me further in.
Birthing is not an easy process,
even as a metaphor.

Instinctively, my body knows,
the bodies of thousands before me;
we all remember.
We are creators, it is our birth right,
a fertile place where life starts again.

When we create something in us dies,
it cannot be otherwise, we transform, in an instant.
Change calls, we listen, with open hands,
shedding.

Safety does not come from building walls of hardened stone and hiding any longer,
protection from feeling is based in misguided preference and doubt,
don't believe the lies they tell you!
You can fall apart.

It is perfectly fine to be neither fine nor perfect,
your weeping, wailing, grief and praise that is the gift.
Your presence unwraps tarnished paper scribed with stories of old,
your body, the paper, polished through tears.

That new babe comes out crying,
and you are there, receive her,
spirit in body, she can be anything.

Tell her of your wisdom,
unlock secrets of potential and give to her freely,
remind her that she is a creator and can destroy worlds,
affirm it is of her choosing and that there is no right choice.

Go beyond boxes of good and bad towards her moral compass within -
that place knows the way of heart.
Encourage her to become intimate with her feet;
they form a foundation from which she grows courage.
Teach her of discrimination so she may trust in her knowing always.

When she has a hunch of insight, let her receive the victories,
neither comdemn or critique her mistakes,
rather let lessons and learnings be discovered.
Don't coddle her for she is strong,
when you see her in that strength you are a clear mirror,
a mirror that shows her she is all of herself,
complete and whole.

Guide her towards her heart where the only stones are pillars,
for an altar of She who dances there.
Encourage her to sing aloud her song, to expose her deepest longings,
to offer them in totality with or without hesitation.

Give.

Transition

I pray for smooth transitions
like waves in the ocean,
returning,
receding.
She receives each,
knowing they never left,
they are herself expressing in form,
lifting,
crashing.
As golden retrievers play in water
necklaces strung of tulsi float…
beads to pray on,
to worship her Sakti.

I walk against the current,
to learn challenges that come with resistance to what is,
deciding in time to stop denying and be carried.

To end is to begin,
exposing the seed,
the next step equally as important
as the rest.

A Home Created

Divine mother intervenes
what is beyond justifying
the honest answer:
It is time to open!
Heart, eyes, and ears
to hear what is being asked:
return to center,
shed your skins,
a house is only walls, floor, and roof;
a home is what's created
by intention, understanding, and love.

Temple of Light

In white petals of the lotus,
that come together forming a spaceship to the moon,
I board and birth and become,
I dance there with her,
humbly, trying figure things out,
restless and committed,
She knows the steps already,
I look right and observe,
matching my shape to her form.

The rhythm is changing,
fruits ripen on the vine,
it is a time for harvest,
to collect and receive with gratitude,
as the season alters again,
I put my prayers out and wait.

Trying to Find Truth in Battle

Sweet grass is burning,
four braids in a half moon,
where do I find them?
Those golden laces of hope, of prayer,
on a peninsula of red rocks I follow smoke in the air.

I find him too, or he finds me,
that traveller type on a bike appearing confused.
Where do I go from here?
What is my clarity?
I've gotten myself in too deep to some place I never wanted to be.

My empathy relates to such confusion,
the conflict that feels like a battleground:
grassy fronts all too familiar,
outside a house containing everything once known,
those ways I ask others to tell me answers,
drop me lines, give me clues,
finish my sentences, so I don't have to;
there is no chance of me getting it wrong then…if i don't choose.

It's just like the advice I give unsolicited,
unwarranted, unwanted perhaps,
because who really wants to doubt themselves
and not carve their own path?

My mind cannot answer questions alone.

How do I find instinct?
What does my heart know?
The osprey calls out overhead.

Inheritance

I cover a corpse in a blanket,
with the help of he who started it all,
or perhaps it was the man before him,
another generation back,
another generation back.

Passing on patterns,
like a body that doesn't die,
speaking too softly to hear,
murmuring a thank you and then leaving to find,
something other then
the place that hurts.

A place,
where I can speak my truth when I know it,
and not be smothered by the voices of others
I've asked too many damn times to tell me what to do.

It is in my containment of both,
apparent opposites that can be neither true nor false,
that shift happens.

What is her will?
What is my yes?

I choose.
A choice.

Grief is Praise

Tears streaming become,
creek beds,
where I lye down my troubles,
fears I'll be alone forever
and sadness that accompanies such thought.

Tears streaming become,
waterfalls,
releasing into a pool collecting below,
where I stand upright on rocks
to be reminded of who I am.

Tears streaming become,
rivers,
currents that I walk against only for so long,
before I tire of trying so hard,
when I could be floating downstream.

Tears streaming become,
oceans,
that cut across landscapes and mend horizons,
bringing together what is distant and what is close,
beyond minds understanding.

In the teachers room

She speaks with surety telling me,
it is not purpose that will protect you,
it is light, the spark, the seed,
not writing, nor art, not creating story or song,
that is worship for her Sakti,
a celebration.

Your worth doesn't come from what you do,
or how it is done,
it is who you are that we love.

That right there is enough
to break a heart open,
for all the years lost
in trying to win attention,
gain approval,
and be seen.

You are the gift, she says.

Be the gift.

Disillusioned

It is grief in the recognition
that he is just as fragile as me,
like flowers under a periwinkle sun setting,
we don't know when petals will drop,
or be plucked halfheartedly.

It is grief in the recognition,
that I made him into a knight,
thinking armour might keep me safe,
keep him safe,
from my dark side,
the same dark side he has…
shadows don't discern,
they play tricks until integrated.

It is grief in the recognition
that we hardly saw eye to eye,
because that seemed too scary
to parts and pieces,
scarred scared children,
longing to be loved,
and the anger that covers them
in fire, a distraction.

It is grief in the recognition
that I shut doors,
based on assumptions and denial,
not wanting to admit you weren't perfect,
because that meant I'm not either,
but judgment doesn't have to come with such thought.

It is grief in the recognition
that rather than having faith in myself,
I wanted you,
and in that
I lost you,
and me both,
gaining us in a cage;
hearts don't like to be trapped.

It is grief in the recognition
that these holes within me,
are places where I could have met you
in light peeling layers,
unwrapping to expose,
the centre core,
and loving what's right there.

All I ever wanted
was to be seen in the eyes of love.

Sweet Honey

Hopeless romantic,
caught in the wires of wishing…
if only I could fall in love,
then I would be free.

Where would I be falling?

Into your own lap, she whispers.
Come close,
even closer,
look here.

Kiss your own independent freedom,
a space in you with absolute surety knows:
I am whole.

Such things are not obtainable from another just as forgetful.
That is absurdity.

She smiles, knowing of such intimacy;
a sweet honey nectar that breaks bondage.

You Never Were

I have given you,
dolls dressed in elegance,
animals stuffed with hope,
statues that sit on shelves,
watching,
as this all begins to unfold.

What will remain when
bricks of dread and disappointment,
of vulnerability and protection,
feelings far from the shore,
throw me out,
caste to a sea of betrayal and abandonment...
what will happen when they are gone?

Was it ever you?

How much I outsource through blame.

It is my power I let go of
in asking you to be the one
to fix these festering wounds,
to answer the endless tiresome questions,
that have you running
towards an island off in the distance,
no where to be found.

I go to that island and find myself surrounded by water, thirsty.
I take a sip.
I jump in.

I've been Dreaming

I've been dreaming you
in my imagination
to be something
you never could be,
with a hope
if you became
him with the golden key
I wouldn't have to unlock my own traps.

The pain of realizing
our love was an illusion
of expectations ever greater each day
breaks my heart
into something more real
then what we shared as fantasy.

At least with pain,
there can be understanding
beyond projections and lofty ideas,
bringing me into an aching heart
as delusions slip away
on the next outgoing breathe.

You never were my answer,
you never were the problem,
you are, just like me,
looking for answers to problems created all to close to home.

Going out instead of going in.
You, the creator, can destroy.

Bride of the Water

She dives into the sea,
surrounded by a rhythm that knows itself and celebrates her in being
a bride of the water,
the one who wears her own ring,
pearl of longing, developed in darkness,
in the deep, almost out of reach,
until it emerges, polished.

She wears it proudly,
honoring the promise,
to a goddess in green dancing,
to one who wears red, poised in her own nature,
a protector of light,
to She cloaked in black walking her into
an unknown place
where fire towers break
and burn in transformation.

Grace arrives in wishing trees seeding,
soon to bear fruit,
triangles intersect forming something new,
elephants stomp a firm ground,
look, up! towards an open sky,
spotted with stars that speak of infinity,
as eternal as love,
that is the place where guidance
descends.

Listen.
I am.

Dream lover

I am not a damsel in distress
that needs your rescue
any longer,
the beast in me
knows of her own beauty
without you saying it as such
or finding a shoe that fits.

I would rather be savaged
with my feet on the earth
feeling rock and moss,
looking up at tree tops,
where nests are built and birds fly,
than wearing what isn't mine
so you can call me
princess bride.

I am not here to be owned
by your magic and spells,
that turn pumpkins into chariots,
when midnight strikes on the clock tower,
he who climbs woven braids
towards a castle in my mind
the man that isn't broken and doesn't cry is just a lie,
that has him trying all to hard
to stay solid like steel and stone,
with an excuse to be alone
and a need to be needed
that no longer serves
them becoming their own.

Fairytales fooled me into believing
to be liked you must be nice,
it's a dream lover
that stays far away
from a heart
of all colors,
the whole rainbow not just snow white.

Won't you come closer
so we can dance in the rain,
naked and vulnerable,
without a need to prove
how much
i love you,
just for you.

Weave

Two threads weave together,
stitching up the staircase of my spine,
merging, parting in separation,
around a column of light
defined yet ever expanding.

The paradox doesn't make sense
for a mind that tries to find containers
for something far too alive.

She tells me,
don't be too demonstrative with your emotions
then he doesn't learn how to feel.
Fires burn, leaving a bed of coals and prayer filled ashes,
deconstructing density,
transforming wood and stone.

Peaceful waters remain,
where swans swim at the heart interweaving,
touch and let go, gracefully,
rise towards a spacious sky,
returning to embody,
your greatest gift and the challenge of non-attachment.

Joy is not something that can be captured,
or was ever meant to be.

She tells me,
develop your own two selves,
harmonize with aspiration, for an endless journey awaits.

If one half is too strong and moves forward
the other lags behind.
Find balance in between.

Where do I need cultivation?
What hopes to be refined?

She tells me,
you are complete already,
having all that you need,
it is only forgetfulness that has you misguided,
a mindless blip of eternity.

You are it all, you see,
free.

Light

Here in between two worlds,
a medial walker with many questions,
humble; at other times thinking I know.
Still, to climb the mountain,
to pause in place,
reminding that ever forgetful self,
this is who you are:
not the body,
not the mind,
light eternal,
luminous effervescent light.

How many times can I neglect my essence?
How often I draw a blank,
handfuls multiplied by a thousand,
and still that does not touch the Truth.

Does Light care if I remember?
Dancing in those moments I do,
She dances, and again I go to sleep,
all so quick,
her patience could follow worlds turning through time slowly,
her love omnipresent, a healing force,
abundance offered generously,
there is no such thing as withholding,
a gift becomes such when given.

How much mercy does it take for wounds of unworthiness to mend?
Such stories, don't they tire of themselves, sensing,

there is something more than this.
That cosmic play; her Lila, great Mother's mystery,
like the ocean, captivates.

Thoughts spinning on repeat, infantile, yet seeming larger than life,
that is the illusion we are here to fight,
until a realization arrives:
attachment stifles peace and equanimity.

What could my world be if I truly believed,
down in the deep of my bones,
each and every one,
cell by cell in celebration,
that I am surrounded by Light!

What created me will sustain me.
Will I give it a chance?

It's just This

Again, I stand in place,
tension courses through my body,
exhale and relax, a new beginning,
the start of recognizing miracles
enveloping me, suffusing me,
the extra-ordinary is what's ordinary.

A spark of illumination reveals:
you are not here to ponder others,
it is of no use to compete or compare,
the outside is merely appearance.
Withdraw to discover,
your mind, a creator,
imagination, a tool or torment,
use it wisely and with intent.

Dreams too easily obstruct reality,
wishful thinking and fantasy far off in the distance
stalk close behind.
This could be enough if you let it;
to accept doesn't mean stagnation.

Don't miss the good for wanting something better,
desire is ever hungry through the night.
The grass is greener where you water it
not on the other side of the hill,
where contentment may be found too,
someplace, elsewhere.
Life happens here, not over there.

It is not purpose that protects you,
what you do does not define you,
the map is your heart that has all the keys.

Proving meaning is not one of them.

Unmasked Imperfection

You. Simple, frazzled, not perfect nor needing to be, you.
Messy, unkept, organized, cautious, cold, you.
Fearful, faithful, scattered, devoted, joyful, you.
You are the gift -
you do not have to strive, to show, to put on display,
to walk around repenting,
for yesterdays shortcomings or today's,
it is enough to just be;
relax and breathe,
surrender together with an act of will.

The Holy House

Separation, segregation,
a feeble attempt to keep track of aspects
each having their own demands,
oh, it will leave you rigid and uncomfortable!

Integrate,
come to accept the foes inside,
make friends with your version of
resistance and sorrow,
terror and damaged trust,
overwhelm knocking loudly,
interrogation and shameful secrets,
indignation, blame, and pain.
Welcome them each!
There is so much to learn from what's been in hiding,
the outcast has a gift to give if you will listen.

To be imperfect doesn't make you broken,
it makes you human.
Truth knows
you are whole.

The outcast whispers,
seeds can be scarred and still grow.

Star

Stars hang against a darkened sky like crystal chandeliers.
Where is that light within me?
Light that captures the attention of fleeting thoughts,
putting into perspective our sheer insignificance and our miracle,
a gift, it is, to be human embodying the Divine!

What is that light that continues to shine long after it has passed into a void?
Leaving behind a legacy for others to ponder and start a fire within,
a spark of insight and inquiry.

How did I get here?
When did I arrive?
Where do I go when I leave?
Was this planned by appointment?

Meaning, I am meant to be,
right here, right now,
that idea could change worlds.
Do you believe it?

Star 2

I look up and small suns twinkle
appearing to stretch themselves into infinity
without even trying.
I confuse crickets for blades of grass,
weary from all my efforts,
to be something more.

Do stars set out to be radiant?
Does fire work itself tired to burn bright?
Isn't it enough to let the river of her love course through these veins?
She knows how – her essence, movement and Light.

It doesn't have to be so hard to love.
It doesn't have to be so hard to love.
When the clouds are peeled back
there are still stars, shining.

Ruthless

Truth is not always easy,
not coated in rainbows and glistening jewels.
Sometimes it comes like an unexpected downpour,
a diamond in the rough unpolished,
not polite nor trying to be,
for sugared coatings, niceties, ass kissing, and trying to please,
does little for evolution's course.

Seed Return

Ember rouses itself
into a flame that consumes insecurities,
hindrances to growth.

Some seeds need to be scorched
before becoming,
emergent.

Adaptation supports growth,
roots reaching a little here, a little there,
accommodating all types of weather,
adjust, they do, accordingly,
trying to secure in shaky ground.

Are we not like seeds?
Full of latent possibilities,
elemental forces playing under a sky,
in discovery as they uncover
their essential selves.
That's where we are headed.

A peach seed will not sprout apples,
Cherry will not be Pine,
What becomes of a seed of Light?

Eventually, we find our way,
star seeds fallen from sky,
sinking themselves into a body down on earth,
this classroom where we learn how growth happens.

It isn't always easy, is it?
Unrealistic thoughts deem it should be so.
The challenges of being all too contained and knowing it,
what does one do with such knowledge?

It is inevitable,
when the time is right the seed sprouts,
the return begins.

Uncertainty

Certainty, what certainty?
Life is a verb you see,
asking for your responsibility,
to be the one who sets yourself free
already, you are, just be,
the confusion complicates simplicity,
obstructing the basis of reality into fantasy.

There is no life in the deadened mechanics of thinking,
oh I know,
you are,
this way,
and always will be.
I am,
that way,
and never could be.

I call bullshit
on the lies and sweet nothing lullabies that have been rocking me to sleep,
on the niceties and petty I'm sorry's,
confining a heart into staying liked.

Validation is like a loaded gun,
approval like a broken pot,
trying to be filled,
meanwhile, draining and denying,
how scary it seems to be that radiant.

Luminous.

Captivating.
Unpredictable.
Dynamic.
Self.

Break

It is life that happens when too busy making plans,
jumping from here to there,
catapulted off into the distance,
on a teeter totter, clinging on, hold tight
run away, I think I might,
to some place else where the earth doesn't tremble,
like fear in my heart in recognition:
I am not in control here.
It shakes like wings of a butterfly discovering itself.

That same butterfly,
developed in a chrysalis of darkness
expands its beauty to float on currents of the next most suitable choice.

This soul merging with its very own self,
oh, divine love!
the nectar of immortals dripping with the sweetest sap.

That is the type of life I long for...
when I don't know is an answer
of assurance
and truth matters more than false facts.

When the unknown is not braced for
but rather embraced
yes!

Now,
this is all there is.
Who said I needed to get it right?

Blocked

When storm clouds pass over
and smoke from fires burning on distant mountain tops
cover a blue sky in grey,
does spaciousness disappear?

In moments when I disregard,
ignore my holy nature,
that divine essence, spark of light,
does it too vanish in my fear?

It couldn't,
what I am, in truth,
go away,
would it?

Desert a seeker of sincerity,
in her heartbreak of forgetting
and longing to remember?

O, this tiny body,
containing the limitlessness in so many limitations.

It must not be possible,
it just isn't so,
that she would ignore one who is hurting,
Her mercy and care is grander
than the screen blocking my clear sight,
than my emotions keeping me blind,
than the resentment towards my own inadequacies.
Is she laughing or praying,

knowing all along,
my true home never looses its sanctum
as wicked winds blow.

She is,
carried by such marvel,
that has me spinning and falling to the ground.
She spins and spins just like the wind,
wheels turning round.

Scapegoat

I will not forsake thee
only in my delusions when again I believe,
for comforts sake,
I...
I couldn't possibly...
it wouldn't be alright if I were
so absolutely
FREE.

If I were too be luminous
shining like ten thousand stars in a blackened sky,
like sun giving rise to shadow,
the light and darkness,
merging, dancing,
major and minor scales in unity,
create a harmonic that calls forth
siva's destruction and compassion both.

She can welcome it all,
allowing the orphan, the sage, the devil, the menace,
in her womb of creation everything is included.

There is nothing I need to push away,
and that doesn't mean the embrace will not answer
in clarity's conviction for evolution's sake:
NO
no longer
no longer am I going
no longer am I going to let you believe
such thoughts that you are

anything less than beautiful,
imperfect
So what?
Who says?
Sincerity of heart is the key.

A paradoxical balance
of heavenly and horrendous,
how could it be otherwise?
Why should it be otherwise?

When the battle is fought and courage is discovered,
the inner strength like a gem in an empty room,
then I will show you that the battle was nothing but play,
for your resilience to be revealed and your essence honored.

Love Requires Everything

Why be so afraid of love?
Where are the roots of your fear?
Can you follow them to the start?
Digging to the deepest tendril,
What do you find there?

Do you know this is all you've ever wanted?
to be loved and to love,
returning limitations five by one,
for a free fall into the water,
ocean of bliss,
is that it?
The root of this fear,
knowing you must get in, swim, dive to the depths of
darkness,
to retrieve what is yours.

That pearl of a great price resides on the sea floor,
it asks you to be enveloped by a power greater than you could
conceive,
the force of love is all you need.
It is impossible to stand on the shoreline and receive the ring.
Your commitment depends on your very own exploring.

Leap!

It's a total loss of control,
No more questions can stall you now,
to renounce this sense of you and me,
you jump,
merging with waves,
the current that carries you through terrors wake,
the many forms resistance to love takes,
must be faced and given away.

Look straight at what surfaces in the process of loosing yourself.
Who is that that you deem to call you?
Is it true?
Couldn't it be that everything you have believed,
about what you are and how you are meant to be was accepted blindly,
all too early,
and is, in reality, nothing but false prophecy,
love as your essence is here to set you free.
That same love you've developed ten thousand ways to push away.

That causes the heart to shake, doesn't it?
Small me, wrong me,
bad me, poor me,
me, me, look at me,
excuses that limit infinity.

Yes, you, are, that big.
And that is the request,

to shine on like a diamond,
unlocking chains that confine
love from dancing with itself outside of the lines.

Is that what is frightening?
Those moments when "you" disappear?
If only you could see with clarity what becomes of your pain
then,
you might be blinded by such light,
you might be consumed by fire,
flames that transform,
and dismantle locks at the doors of your heart.

Love, asks of your everything
and gives to you eternity.

Bloom

Does the Iris hesitate to open when time calls?
Withholding her own evolution in fearfulness?
To expose the essence is a natural progression of things living under the sun.

The lily, isn't she here to unfurl her petals,
to reveal her true humble beauty,
to be touched by the wings of hummingbirds and moths,
opening colored runways for bees to discover that sweet nectar taste,
and then, one by one, renouncing attachments,
she drops her petals, spreads her seed,
leaving gifts for the next generations yet to arrive.

What is contained within a seed?
Have you ever stopped to wonder?
What helps things to grow, to become?

Is it an unavoidable fact of life,
that we eventually blossom into our full potential,
whether we'd prefer it to be that way or not,
inevitability summons us there and it becomes to tiring to do otherwise.

Do children wait for flowers to bloom?
Aren't we most happy when they do?

Then why,
Why is it you and I would think to not match summers clarion call;

She sends it forth again, each season reminding us,
"You either are full, or looking to be filled,
You either love, or demand love to you,
Be like a flower in bloom."

Uprooted

In the course of securing predictability,
missed are opportunities to wonder,
what is this longing for certainty?
How has it gained such momentum?
When did it start trying to determine what will be?

There are corners in my mind like bedrooms where I grew,
full of dust bunnies and monsters in closets,
fairies and avatars tall and blue;
they never truly did exist; only in my imagination.
Imagination, a hindrance hurling us into story lines untrue…
Imagination, a power when directed with intent.

There are pinpoints of sensations wedged in chambers of my heart,
they wake me in dream with memories,
a feeling of sadness hard to describe,
my faith in the unknown demands my attention to the cries,
om tara, her compassion, my lullaby.

I, myself, didn't wish to be dismissed into definition,
a deadening idea of "you are" and "this is",
like putting a plant into a cardboard box and telling it "grow",
limited space makes for limited expansion,
and how then does light get it?

Demanding answers too quickly dulls what is dynamic,
disturbs roots long since anticipating,
already pushing through unconscious worlds,
restlessness distracts me from feeling…
a fear of missing out.

What if the world was my fallow field,
and I the field, farmer, and seed alike,
would I try to make accusations of what will happen with my life,
or tend, with presence and care, what wishes for growth?

Mapped

There are two wings that help me lift,
one is Father, the other, Mother,
both of Divine stature,
the formless birthed into beauty through form.
Why would I fear such energy?
The energy that gave me life and keeps me alive,
how could I not celebrate its' very existence?
Receptivity, listening, devotion, admiration, and love,
flowers of the rainbow, their petals open in wonder of all there is.
Oneness.

Awesome in the truest sense of the word is the tip of the iceberg.
The rest cannot be said, only felt,
an experience waxing and waning like phases of the moon.

Something remains beyond changing expressions,
that which nourishes my growth,
that which could not be contained, and yet, is.
I am the container already in full supply.
The moments I search outside to try and find is the moment I deny.

What keeps me from taking responsibility?
The potential to misuse is by no means wrong,
only lacking refinement, discrimination, and follow-through.
Deeper, what's underneath that answer?
Beyond what first comes to the mind.

If I accepted I am stars and Light,
a hallow vessel filed with beliefs and stories never real,
I would loose all I know.

Is that it?
What I have considered myself to be is only,
at most, a fraction divided again.
Something remains and I want to stand with that.
The essence of all things cannot go away;
only its' container,
this life, not Light.

No right answers

A mirror,
still lake reflection revealing myself
to the one who looks;
I am as I am.

Life is not a test I take to get right answers;
always go for C if you don't know,
that was my motto,
scribble something in pencil just light enough on those wooden desks,
keep the paper between my legs out of view,
the notes on my hands covered,
so the teacher can't see me cheating,
to try to be correct;
that deep fear of failure
cloaked in pride and hiding.

Confusion is a saving grace
that keeps me from thinking
I know what I do not
certainty stealing wonder;
there is no time for that,
class is over.

The rest of us,
we may pretend to have ourselves together,
standing on stable ground and spinning with momentum,
holding on breathe by breathe,
unwilling to admit truth even to ourselves,
that truth that cuts through such shows

of what is done to stay liked and in control.

It is devastating to destroy illusions
that have firmly been bought into,
and yet freedom demands it.

When I wake up
I no longer believe
those subliminal messages
that entered my subconscious
before I knew how to differentiate
and discern what is real from lies.
I'm still learning.

In this process of awakening
there is no way to pass or fail,
get things right or get them wrong,
such thinking leads to perfection performing,
an angel in disguise,
or doubt that cripples me from trying.
I look out.

There is no better or worse ways to move forward,
there are paths and there is choice,
what keeps me in movement towards my ideals, towards my God?
I look in.

There are no golden stars of praise for my insecurity,
and no way that such 5 cent stickers could heal wounds of lifetimes,
it couldn't be so easy, as to come from another;

I would be robbed of my victory if it were.

They don't have my answers,
unless questions are multiple choice,
and rules are general and apply to all;
there is far too much possibility for that,
and instinct does not know of regulations.

Until done,
it is not about completion,
this poignant moment,
suspends me like never before,
in a medial space where I reside
with projections of security that blind me from seeing
such uncertainty full of potential.

Will I grab onto something familiar?
What, right now, can be born?
It's all to easy to become comfortable,
to slip into what spins automatic,
the battle begins when I stop and start again.

This life is very precious,
a gift for the soul to see itself,
in mirrored reflections of eternal moments.

Time,
the devil,
another delusion trying to keep me on track,
playing games with something
way bigger than it could ever be.

My world, my choosing, my responsibility.
What do I want to create?

Humility, strikes me, in worship.
I cannot get it wrong,
free to move forward,
taking the next step.

Timeless

If it doesn't amend now,
it will;
the journey may be different,
if you go left and not straight,
or walk down crooked paths,
but,
I'm not ready,
until I'm ready,
and my soul has time.

May that not be an excuse,
to stay stuck in mud,
but an aspiration
to become
like the lotus petals
opening
to 18 kinds of knowledge.

Seeded Body

I am more like a seed than this body,
if I speak in metaphor loosely,
this body contains all the seed represents,
my spiritual tool for evolution,
and still, it is not who I am.

Under my skin there are universes I have yet to think of,
unimaginable to my minds limitations,
there are galaxies I cannot see and still they glisten,
stars of whom I know few,
and she who stands at their edge guiding me back home.

There are pairs of opposites that merge and separate
for their own amusement,
providing me with lessons and learning.
There is a vast endless source of something I cannot name, only feel,
and still it is real beyond understanding in the way we so often do.

There are secrets and whispers,
a small voice I hear offering unbiased wisdom and truths,
of cutting compassion that needs to be said.

There, rests the dark side of the moon awaiting my approach,
patiently, with encouragement as I walk straight and down idle paths,
there are elements rearranging themselves in each instant,
earth, water, fire, air, and space as I learn it is okay
to be empty with recognition I am already full.

Between heaven and earth I discover the essential me.

She takes form as a shadow side to the sun,
a darkness where pause happens without doing anything,
and ignorance is persuaded to chase fleeting images on concrete.
It is by the suns reflection we grow up.

Who are you? Nothing finite is true.
The seed is potential emerging.
Kinetic, dynamic, latent and yet trying to be.

The flower, oak, and cherry each have a purpose to fulfill,
authenticity finds them eventually, until then,
each step is an unfolding mystery in response to subtle shifts.

That is the beauty of life.
How it is cultivated in moments by choice and still has a plan in mind.
Fate and free-will dancing together graceful in their return.

Time to be holy

There comes a time to be holy,
to see what seems broken, incomplete, not free,
as already whole entirely.
Others can, in no way, fulfill that space of forgetting who you are.
It isn't up to them nor possible to come from outside.
It is your destiny in the making; one very precious life.
What do you choose?
How do you remember what is easily denied for comforts sake?
A child of God, gift from the Goddess,
all things marvellous and dangerous; to stand as a beacon of Light,
what might that give you?
Taken is what keeps you small and pretending,
over-identified with an actor,
for heaven's sake of your own greatness,
let it be so.
Give up what you hold too close.
The only call to answer is your own.

www.ingramcontent.com/pod-product-compliance
Lightning Source LLC
Chambersburg PA
CBHW030457010526
44118CB00011B/978